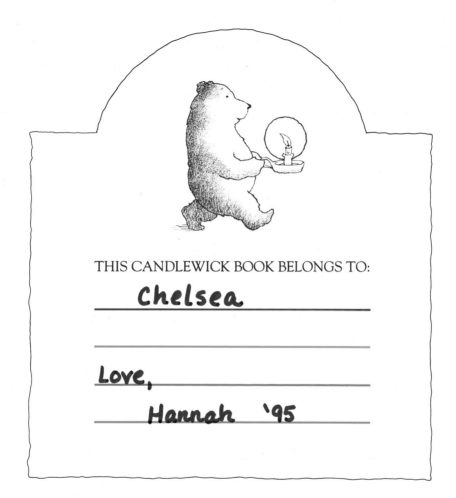

THIS CANDLEWICK BOOK BELONGS TO:

Chelsea

Love,

Hannah '95

For William

P. A.

First U.S. edition 1994
Published in Great Britain in 1994 by
Walker Books Ltd., London.

Library of Congress Cataloging-in-Publication Data

Ayres, Pam, 1947–
Guess where? / written by Pam Ayres ; illustrated by Julie Lacome.—
1st U.S. ed.

Summary: Presents questions which can be answered by looking at
the illustrations, such as "This poor sheep is in despair, her
naughty lamb is hiding . . . where?"
ISBN 1-56402-314-1
[1. Picture puzzles. 2. Stories in rhyme.]
I. Lacome, Julie, ill. II. Title.
PZ8.3.A96Gt   1994
[E]— dc20   93-24336

10 9 8 7 6 5 4 3 2 1

Printed in Hong Kong

The pictures in this book were done in paper collage.

Candlewick Press
2067 Massachusetts Avenue
Cambridge, Massachusetts 02140

Guess Where

Pam Ayres

illustrated by
Julie Lacome

CANDLEWICK PRESS
CAMBRIDGE, MASSACHUSETTS

Bubbles right up
to my chin—
did I put my
hippo in?

Tiger's lost
beneath the trees!
Will you help to find
him, please?

We love going
on the bus.
Where do you think
it's taking us?

This poor sheep is
in despair.
Her naughty lamb is
hiding . . . where?

Bread and honey
in the shade—
do you know where
honey's made?

My hand's warm in
Mommy's pocket.
Can you see a fiery
rocket?

Poor old Molly
looks so sad.
Where's the tasty
bone she had?

A fire engine races through! Where can it be going to?

A spider's web all wet with dew— can you see the spider too?

Can you see my
yellow ball?
It floated down
the waterfall!

At the ocean
can you spy
a star that is not
in the sky?

We like the park!
We love the swings!
Where are all your
favorite things?

PAM AYRES has published books of poems, recorded albums, and even had her own television show. She is the author of several books for children, including *When Dad Cuts Down the Chestnut Tree* and *When Dad Fills in the Garden Pond*. Pam Ayres lives in an old vicarage in Oxfordshire, England, with her husband, two sons, and an assortment of sheep, ducks, geese, chickens, and a cat and a dog.

JULIE LACOME graduated with a degree in graphic design and illustration. Also the illustrator of *A Was Once an Apple Pie* by Edward Lear, and the author-illustrator of *Walking Through the Jungle* and *I'm a Jolly Farmer*, Julie Lacome is currently a free-lance artist and art teacher.

Other Candlewick books by Pam Ayres and Julie Lacome:

Guess What
Guess Who
Guess Why